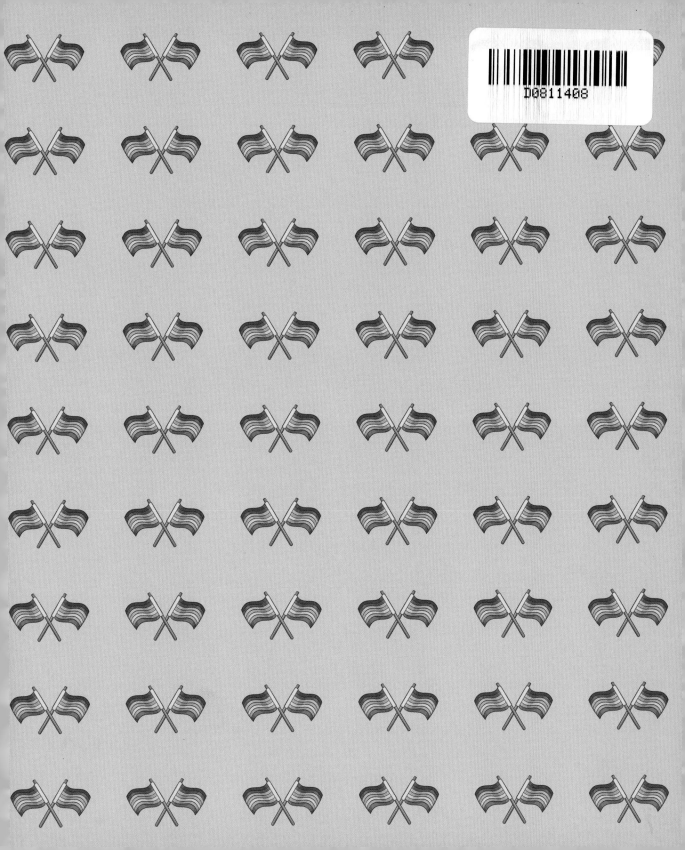

UNDERSTANDING
SEXUALITY

What it means to be lesbian, gay or bisexual

HONOR HEAD

W

FRANKLIN WATTS

LONDON•SYDNEY

Franklin Watts
First published in Great Britain in 2017 by The Watts Publishing Group

Credits:
Series Editor: Jean Coppendale
Series Designer: Lorraine Inglis
Consultants: Dr Michael Halls and Andy Hunt at Intercom Trust

Picture credits:
Every attempt has been made to clear copyright. Should there be any inadvertent omission please apply to the publisher for rectification.
t = top, b = bottom, l = left, r = right, m = middle
Cover: © Shutterstock/marrishuanna
All images listed here are © of Shutterstock and: 4t Mad Dog, b PsheNa; 6bl Chombosan; 7b Emolaev Alexander; 8t Castelski; 10 Cienpies Design; 11t S_Binkley, m Mochipet; 12 flag Trifonenkolvan; 13 rainbow door Maeblys; 18-19 background Itamara, 19 pimchawee; 20m Featureflash Photo Agency, b Irina Adamovich; 20/21 flags vectorok, 21t Philip Chidell; 22 dovia982; 23m dominika zarzycka, b Creatarka; 24 artbesouro; 25l emran, tr SLDesign; 26-27 AVABitter; 27tr Helga Esteb; 28-29 background, kampolz, birds, Mrs. Opossum.

Note to parents and teachers: Every effort has been made by the Publishers to ensure that these websites are suitable for children, that they are of the highest educational value, and that they contain no inappropriate or offensive material. However, because of the nature of the Internet, it is impossible to guarantee that the contents of these sites will not be altered. We strongly advise that Internet access is supervised by a responsible adult.

ISBN 978 1 4451 5216 5
Printed in China

MIX
Paper from responsible sources
FSC
www.fsc.org
FSC® C104740

Franklin Watts
An imprint of
Hachette Children's Group
Part of The Watts Publishing Group
Carmelite House
50 Victoria Embankment
London EC4Y 0DZ

An Hachette UK Company
www.hachette.co.uk

www.franklinwatts.co.uk

Contents

What is sexuality? 4

Time for change 6

What is LGB? 8

Same-sex crush 10

Setting the record straight! 12

Coming out 14

Homophobia – it's bad! 16

Bad feelings 18

Religion and LGB 20

Sex! 22

Same-sex families 24

Proud to be me! 26

So, to recap 28

Glossary 30

Further information 31

Index 32

WHAT IS SEXUALITY?

Sexuality is not just about sex, it's about how you interact with others, your values, how you see yourself and what and who you find attractive.

Values and expectations

Basically, sexuality describes your romantic and sexual feelings for another person. But it is much more than that. The way we were brought up and our family and community values have a huge effect on how we handle sexual and romantic relationships with other people. Our expectations of other people, and what we pick up from the media also affect our sexuality.

We're all different

As you grow into young adults you begin to explore your own personal and sexual identity. You discover what sort of people you get on with and what physical characteristics you like, such as black hair or blue eyes. Some people find members of the opposite sex attractive, while others are attracted to their own sex or to both men and women. Finding someone attractive sexually isn't just about what they look like or what sex they are, it's about what you have in common, how well you get on and how comfortable and safe you feel being with them.

Sexuality and LGB

Sexuality is a huge subject so in this book we are dealing with lesbian, gay and bisexual sexuality, what that means and how it affects us all. Being lesbian, gay or bisexual means being sexually attracted to and having feelings for people of the same sex as yourself or for both sexes. Being heterosexual or straight means having sexual feelings for people of the opposite sex only. Some people become asexual; that is, they don't have any sexual feelings at all, but they can still feel close to people and have deep feelings for someone. They just don't express them in a physical way.

Whether you find people of your own sex attractive or people of the opposite sex or both is called your sexual orientation. In most countries society accepts that there are many different ways to live your life so that you can be true to your feelings.

TALKBACK!

Look out for the TALKBACK boxes. This is where you and your friends, family or classmates can discuss two sides of an argument. There are no right or wrong answers, but you might be surprised at the conclusions you come to.

Time for change

Your sexuality develops as you become a teenager and grow into an adult. Puberty and adolescence mark the move from childhood to adulthood.

Puberty and adolescence

During puberty your body begins to develop and change as you become an adult. The average age for the start of puberty for girls is 11 and for boys 12, but this can happen any time between the ages of 8 and 14. Girls begin to grow breasts as they develop a more womanly shape, and their periods start. Boys develop a deeper voice, their testicles grow, and their bodies start to become more muscular. All young people will begin to sweat more and develop body hair.

Adolescence is usually said to begin when you become a teenager. Between the ages of 13 and 19 you may experience a growth spurt and physical changes will continue as your body becomes fully adult.

There's more?

As if all this growing and changing wasn't bad enough, puberty and adolescence can play havoc with your emotions and feelings. This is because your body is going through hormonal changes. Many young people begin to question how they fit in with their peers, friends and family. Emotions become more intense and moods can swing about from one extreme to another. You might feel angry, restless, weepy, scared and just plain confused. This is normal. Some young people don't experience any of this, and that's ok, too!

Strange feelings

During puberty and adolescence you might start to feel strong physical and mental attractions to other people. When you are younger you might develop a crush and want to be with one person all the time. If you are older, you might start to feel a strong physical attraction to another person. This can seem a bit strange to begin with but these feelings are nothing to be ashamed or scared of. Sexual feelings are not dirty or bad for you. In our pre-teen and teen years we begin to explore what interests us sexually and what our sexual orientation is. We discover the type of people we like and what we find attractive in others.

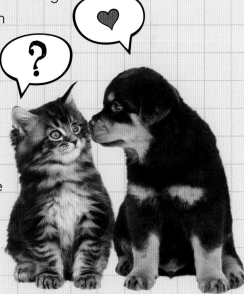

WHAT IS LGB?

LGB stands for lesbian, gay and bisexual. It is a respectful way to refer to people who are not heterosexual.

The basics

Most people think of a traditional couple as a man and a woman. But today we accept that this is not so straightforward. Some men find other men attractive or like both men and women. Some women find other women attractive or like both women and men. If you think that you are lesbian, gay or bisexual you should not have to feel embarrassed, scared or ashamed of this, but many young people are. You should be able to expect the support of your family, friends and school, but being LGB can still be very challenging.

Can we choose to be LGB?

People can experiment with their sexuality but if someone is gay or lesbian or straight that is just how they are. You can't make yourself homosexual and if you're LGB you can't make yourself straight. There are some people who say that counselling or psychotherapy or even medical help can 'cure' homosexuality, but homosexuality is not a mental or physical illness. It is perfectly natural and doesn't just exist in humans … in nature many animals form same-sex relationships.

LGBTQ+

There is an even longer set of initials. The letters stand for:

- L = lesbian. This is a woman who is sexually attracted to other women.
- G = gay. This is usually a man who is attracted to other men.
- B = bisexual. A person who is attracted to both men and women.
- T = transgender. This refers to a person who feels that they don't identify with the gender they were born with. For example, a child with male genitals and given the gender 'boy' at birth, may in some cases feel strongly he isn't a boy.
- Q = questioning. This refers to people still questioning their sexual orientation. It can also mean someone unsure of their gender, who feels they may be both male and female and are attracted to men and women as either gender.
- + = anyone who feels they don't fit into any of the above.

The words gay and homosexual are often used as a general term to describe lesbians, gay men and bisexuals.

To be clear...

Gender is not about sexuality. Sexuality is about who you are physically attracted to. Gender is how you feel about who you are, whether you feel you are a boy, a girl, a mix of boy and girl or you change between being a boy and a girl. Transgender people can be gay, heterosexual, lesbian or bisexual.

SAME-SEX CRUSH

Nearly everyone has a same-sex crush at some time in their life. Some of these people are LGB, some are not.

Same-sex crush

This is when you develop very strong feelings for a person of the same sex, and it can happen to girls and boys. You might have a crush on a celebrity or someone at school. A crush is like an infatuation. You become obsessed about the person, fantasise about them, want to be like them and desperately want them to feel the same about you. A crush can make you feel very happy and also sad if the person doesn't feel as you do.

Keep changing

Having a same-sex crush doesn't mean that you are LGB. Crushes are a natural part of growing up and help us to find out what we like and find attractive in others. We change emotionally through adolescence and early adulthood and this includes changes to our feelings for others. Your sexual orientation will develop as you experience more and meet more people. For some people their sexuality never stops changing.

LGB? OK!

If you are LGB, that's great. Today, in many countries (including the UK and Australia), LGB people have the legal right to be safe wherever they are: at home, at school, on the street or at work. In the past, social pressures meant that many LGB people had to pretend to be straight and as a result led very unhappy lives. Nowadays, things are more open and society is more tolerant.

> *If I'd had a little bit more time [less pressure] when I was younger I would have come out, because I would have been comfortable with that. And that's why I think, we're all making the same point, around why we don't push people to come out.*

> Ian Thorpe (b. 1982), Australian Olympic swimming champion

It's private

If you're not sure about your sexual orientation, don't worry. Your feelings, emotions and expectations will change a lot over the next few years. Don't feel you have to say one thing because of mates or peer pressure. Your sexual orientation is private and you don't have to discuss it with family or friends if it makes you feel uncomfortable. If you feel confused, upset, or scared of your feelings, phone a helpline for a chat (see page 31).

Setting the record straight!

There are lots of myths and wrong ideas about people who are LGB.

Stereotypes

Over the years, LGB people have been presented as stereotypes; for example, that all lesbians are masculine, have short hair and always wear trousers, and all gay men are feminine and hate sport. Like everyone else, LGB people are all different. Stereotypes make it easier for people to be prejudiced. If we think of everyone in a certain group as being the same, we don't have to think about them as individuals, which makes it easier to judge them or to be nasty or unkind about them. It also makes it easier for people who are prejudiced to believe that somehow LGB people are different from everyone else, when in fact they are not.

The rainbow flag is a symbol of the LGB community. It is also called the freedom flag. The colours represent the many and varied people who belong to the LGB community.

There are no typical **LGB** people just as there are no typical *heterosexual* people.

Myths about LGB people...

- Homosexual men fancy all other men and homosexual women fancy all other women. This is like saying all heterosexual people fancy all members of the opposite sex. It's silly and wrong!

- Lesbians really want to be men. No! Lesbians are happy being women. They just happen to prefer relationships with other women.

- Homosexuals don't mix with straight people. In the past, and in some communities still, homosexuals have been treated badly so they stick together with like-minded people who understand and accept them. Like everyone else, LGB people make friends with those they feel comfortable being with.

TALKBACK!

We expect women and men to dress and behave in a certain way, and when they don't, we're confused. Is conforming to a stereotype important?

We should be able to express ourselves in any way that makes us feel comfortable, regardless of our gender or sexual orientation. We are all different.

But clothes and how people behave help us to get a feeling for the sort of person they are. Otherwise, how do we know what the person we're talking to is like?

COMING OUT

Coming out means telling those closest to you that you are LGB. This is a big decision and one that each person must make for themselves.

In your own time

Individuals can decide for themselves when they tell anyone they are LGB, and who they tell first. When and how people tell their family and friends will depend a lot on what the family and friends are like. If someone has a family or culture where homosexuality is still considered wrong, they might not say anything at all.

Coming out – family reaction

Family reactions will vary. Some families will be supportive, understanding and encouraging. Some parents may be sad, angry, disappointed, confused or embarrassed, or at least to begin with. They may go into denial and not accept that it is happening. Some parents who want the best for their children might think that living as LGB will mean a life of sadness, rejection and bullying, but in many countries attitudes have changed in the last twenty years so this should not be the case. On the whole, most families will experience a mix of all of these emotions and thoughts.

Friends and peers

Some friends will be totally accepting when you come out, and say they 'guessed' and it's no big deal. Some might be curious and they may want to ask questions that are too personal … you don't have to tell details about yourself if you don't want to. Do what is comfortable for you. Others might be shocked, embarrassed or hostile and may not want to be friends any more. It's hurtful when this happens and it can make you feel angry and depressed. Join an online youth group or local club for LGB people your age so you can discuss your feelings and experiences with people who understand.

Be patient

Telling family or close friends you're gay can be a shock for them, especially if they haven't guessed. Give them time to think about what you've said. It might help to write a letter to them before you talk so they can get used to the news.

If you think your friend or sibling might be LGB, how can you make them feel that you will be supportive?

The best thing to do is let the person know you're ok with gay people.

Stand up for LGB rights if someone is being prejudiced, or at least don't join in.

Don't join in rumours that your friend is gay, especially on social media.

Talk about a book you've read or TV programme you've seen with a gay character who you really like.

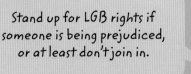

HOMOPHOBIA – IT'S BAD!

Homophobia is a hatred of and discrimination against LGBTQ+ people. It is based on prejudice, fear and ignorance and should not be tolerated.

Bullying

Name-calling, teasing, making jokes about someone, physical harm, spreading rumours about a person's sexuality, ignoring them on social media and threatening to out them is all bullying. Making casual jokes about gay people, how they dress or look or behave, might seem harmless, but it can have a devastating effect. It can make the person being bullied feel scared, humiliated, isolated and worthless and lead to serious situations, which may include self-harming and feelings of suicide.

Your rights

Like everyone else, LGB people have a legal right to feel safe at home, at school and in the community. If you are being made to feel guilty or ashamed at home or being bullied at school or by your family, tell a teacher or trusted adult what is happening. If one teacher will not support you, go to another teacher or phone a helpline. You don't have to admit to being gay or deny being gay to stop the bullying. The bullying should be stopped simply because it is bullying.

Be supportive

Friends and classmates can do a lot to help LGB people feel included and safe. Don't put up with anti-gay insults or people saying the word 'gay' as a bad or negative word. Ask people who make nasty remarks why they're doing it. Mostly young people pick up negative attitudes from their families, the media or online and and haven't thought it through for themselves. If you know someone is being bullied, befriend them, walk home with them or sit with them in the playground. Showing support will help anyone who feels isolated and rejected, and might make all the difference to that person.

Smash ignorance!

LGB bullying is often based on ignorance. Get together with others and do an assembly or class talk on famous LGB people past and present or talk about being LGB.

Discuss these ideas on how to help fight homophobic bullies.

Talk to your friends and draw up an anti-bullying charter.

Have a safe zone – a space where people can go to be together and talk through issues. Talk to a supportive teacher who will supervise.

Offer to go with the bullied person to report what is happening. People being bullied are sometimes too terrified to do anything.

Make notes of times and details of any bullying you see and report it to a trusted teacher.

Bad feelings

Nearly everyone worries about the future and how they're going to fit in, but for some LGB young people the future can seem especially bleak.

Worry, worry!

For young people facing the possibility that they might be gay and different from everyone else can be terrifying. It can trigger a range of bad feelings, including anger, confusion, self-loathing and fear. Most young people worry about school, exams, making friends and what the future holds, but some LGB young people might also have to face all of this feeling that they are 'unacceptable', or that their future living as a gay person is going to be really hard. Young LGB people with supportive friends and family are less likely to have these worries and fears.

Being **LGB** should not stand in the way of anyone *achieving* whatever they want to do in life.

Reach out

For those who feel they cannot talk to family and friends, keeping secrets and not being able to share your innermost thoughts or discuss your fears with anyone can be lonely. Contact a helpline (see page 31) or join an online forum where you can share your feelings with others and get support and feedback. Or see if there is a local support group for LGB young people. If you don't want to get involved with the LGB community, take up a sport or hobby that will encourage you to feel more positive and help you to meet lots of different people.

I went into boxing, and I'm bisexual, and I still achieved and performed at the highest level, and I came away with gold and made history, so with that said, anything is possible.

Nicola Adams (b. 1982),
Olympic champion boxer

Be careful!

Never, ever meet up with anyone you chat with online. Never send photos of yourself, especially sexually explicit photos. If comments make you feel uncomfortable or are threatening or nasty, report it to the forum administrator and leave the site. Never share personal details. Most online friends will be genuine, but as with all online sites, be careful and cautious. Use the forums as a way to express your feelings and get positive feedback.

19

RELIGION AND LGB

Different religions and communities have varying views on homosexuality that can affect how people feel about the LGB community.

Accepting

Today, many religions fully accept and respect the LGB community, and being LGB is not a major issue. Many religious leaders provide valuable support and advice for their local LGB communities and some places of worship may even have their own LGB support groups and clubs.

Not so accepting

Some religions do not have such tolerant attitudes towards the LGB community and this can be very difficult for young people and their families who are LGB and religious. In many instances, families and friends will still love and respect the choice of the LGB person, but some may not. Their religion may express the belief that homosexuality is evil, making the young person feel afraid, rejected, guilty and ashamed. If you feel that coming out to your family or community is not a safe option, wait until you feel strong enough or have a network that can support you. Contact a local community LGB network for confidential support.

Your goals

Some deeply religious families might find it difficult to accept that their child is LGB. Try and talk to your family calmly about how you feel and listen to their concerns. See if there is a close family member or teacher who will support you, or look for online support. Being LGB doesn't make anyone bad or unnatural, it just makes them different and others may find this hard to accept. Believe in yourself and your future and focus on your personal goals.

'*If someone is gay and he searches for the Lord and has good will, who am I to judge? We shouldn't marginalise people for this. They must be integrated into society.*'

Pope Francis (b. 1936), Head of the Roman Catholic Church

TALKBACK!

How important is it for a religion to accept everyone?

You can't go against the teachings of your faith. You have to accept what your religion says.

Religions can and should move with the times so they accept everyone.

SEX!

Whatever your sexual orientation, sex should be something that feels safe and that is part of a caring relationship.

Feelings and emotions

Sex is not just about physical involvement. As you grow older you may find you are attracted to people for many different reasons, for example because they make you laugh, they are easy to talk to or they understand your deepest feelings. Kissing, petting or making out with someone of your own sex doesn't mean you're LGB. Likewise, if you feel sexually attracted to someone of the opposite sex now, that doesn't mean you won't develop sexual feelings towards someone of your own sex in the future.

Pornography – it's not real life

Pornography is made with actors being paid to perform certain roles. It can be violent and scary, and often shows sex as being rough and painful. In real life, sex should be part of a trusting, caring relationship where two people enjoy being together and making each other happy. Watching pornography, whether it's gay or straight, gives a very unreal idea of what sex is like.

It's your choice

Cuddling, kissing, touching and other forms of sex are all intimate activities that are in your control. You have a right to choose who, when and how you want to share intimate activities with. Everyone is different and it's up to each person to decide when they feel comfortable sharing intimate experiences. It's against the law to force a person to do anything sexual that they don't want to, whether it's heterosexual or homosexual sex.

The age of consent is the age the law says is legal for young people to have sex (see page 31) and it is the same for heterosexual and homosexual sex. But even when you reach the age of consent, it's against the law to force anyone to do something they don't want to.

> *Everything kinda clicked, everything went right. He really does make me feel safe and happy.*
>
> Tom Daley (b. 1994), Olympic gold medal winner, about his now husband, Dustin Lance Black

Consent – you decide...

Consent is when you give someone permission to do something. This applies to all young people, whether gay or straight. No one – not family, carers, friends, teachers or anyone else – should do anything physical to you that you feel uncomfortable or bad about or don't agree to. If someone puts pressure on you to do something sexual that you don't want to do or don't think is right, you must tell an adult, the police or phone a helpline. Whatever your sexual orientation, your call will be treated with respect and you should not feel embarrassed or ashamed.

Yes

No

NO

SAME-SEX FAMILIES

A traditional family used to be a man, a woman and children. Today families vary a lot, from single-parent families to same-sex couples.

Family time

Nowadays same-sex couples can have children through adoption, donor insemination, surrogacy or foster care. Studies have shown that generally children of same-sex couples grow up much the same as those from other family backgrounds – they are loved, cared for, supported and prepared for a happy and fulfilling life.

Don't understand

Many people still believe that only male and female parents should have children and find it difficult to accept same-sex families. This could be for religious reasons or because they are homophobic and prejudiced. These prejudices are often passed down to their own children who might become bullies at school. Children with same-sex parents who are being bullied should try and talk to the bully and ask them why they are being so unkind. Some may say it's because same-sex relationships are unnatural, but there is nothing unnatural about two people who love each other wanting to spend their lives together to love and raise children.

Family myths

People can have strange ideas about same-sex couples. Some people believe that lesbians cannot be as maternal or love their kids as much as straight women, but there is no evidence to support this view. Also, there is no evidence that children of same-sex parents will grow up to be gay themselves. Some may be gay, but they would have been gay had they been brought up by a male/female couple.

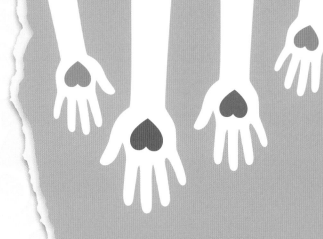

People have babies every day and people have different paths in life. This is mine and I couldn't be more proud of my family and I'm very lucky to have such a great group of people around me.

Casey Dellacqua (b. 1985), Australian tennis champion, on having a baby with her female partner.

Splitting up

Families breaking up is hard enough, but when a parent from a straight couple leaves to live with another partner of the same sex this can be an additional shock for everyone. The children involved should try not to judge either parent, but talk through any anxieties they have with both parents. Don't be embarrassed to talk to your parents about any bullying as a result of the family change. Your parents need to know what is going on so they can help you.

PROUD TO BE ME!

Whether you are gay, straight, bisexual or not sure yet, you are you, unique and special.

Respect!

All young people face challenges as they go through puberty to adulthood, but it can be particularly challenging if you are LGB or think you might be. Being different from your friends and peers can be scary as most people want to fit in and be part of a group. It can be hard but you should respect who you are and your rights and stand up for them. You should also accept the rights of those around you to have mixed feelings about your sexual orientation, as long as they are respectful to you and don't bully or tease you or those who support you.

Be proud

Be proud to be who you are whatever those around you are saying. This is not always easy, but be proud that you had the honesty and courage to admit your true feelings to yourself and, when the time comes, to others.

You're special

You are more than just being LGB. How you treat others, your hobbies, skills, dreams for the future and so much more make you a unique and special person. If you feel you can't come out yet, don't feel guilty or ashamed. Think of the things you enjoy. Build on your skills, plan for your future and enjoy doing your favourite things.

> *Love yourself, whatever makes you different, and use it to make you stand out. Mine is my voice and the fact that I'm gay: well, the fact that I'm flamboyantly gay.*
>
> Ross Mathews (b. 1979),
> US TV personality

Face the challenge

LGB people in some communities might have to face a lot more prejudice and hatred than in others. If you can, build up a supportive network of friends. This might only be a couple of people you know you can trust or a local group. It may take people a while to get used to your news, so be patient, but don't put up with bullying or abuse.

SO, TO RECAP...

This is a recap of the issues we have looked at in this book. They are presented as ideas to discuss. Talking things through can help us to understand ourselves and others a little better and why we react in the way we do in certain situations and to different people.

Homophobic bullying

Any bullying is bad but homophobic bullying is especially nasty. How do you think homophobic bullying makes the LGB person feel? Why do you think people bully LGB people? Bullying is usually based on ignorance and fear – why should people fear LGB people? How can bullies be helped to understand that they don't need to be afraid of LGB people?

Friends and family – be there!

Young LGB people need support to help them face challenging times. Why is this important? How would you support a friend or sibling who was LGB? Would you find it difficult to stand up to the majority if they were against LGB?

LGB stereotypes

There are many stereotypes surrounding LGB people, from masculine lesbians always wearing trousers to gay men hating sport. Why do you think people have these stereotypes? What are they based on? Do they make non-LGB people feel safe?

Same-sex parents

More and more same-sex couples are having children. Do you think children with same-sex parents have the same choices as others? Maybe they have a more tolerant upbringing? Why should they be bullied because they are from a same-sex family?

Sex – it's a thing

This is a big subject that many people feel embarrassed or nervous to talk about. Why do you think this is? Why should sex always be part of a loving, caring relationship? How do you think consent works in a sexual relationship? Why does pornography give us an unreal idea of what a sexual relationship is like?

Religion – right or wrong?

Many people who have a deep faith turn to their religion for support in difficult times. What do you think it must be like for young LGB people who are religious but feel they cannot turn to their faith for support? Why do you think some religions reject LGB people? Do you think it is wrong for a religion to reject young people who might be feeling desperate and lonely?

Glossary

adolescence the time between puberty and adulthood when your body becomes fully grown and developed and you become an adult

asexual a person who has no sexual feelings or desires

denial refusing to believe that something is true because you don't want to admit that it is

donor insemination when sperm from a man who is not the woman's partner is injected into the woman to help her to become pregnant

fantasise to dream about or imagine things that you want to happen but are sometimes not possible

foster care being looked after by foster parents on a temporary basis

gender your own identity as a male, female, both or neither

heterosexual a person who is sexually attracted to people of the opposite sex

homophobia dislike of or prejudice against homosexual people

hostile unfriendly, aggressive and nasty

humiliated to be made to feel ashamed and stupid especially in front of friends or family

interact to talk and do things with other people

intimate to have sexual relations with someone

isolated alone; feeling lonely and that you don't have anyone to turn to and don't belong

marginalise to treat a person or group as if they are unimportant and make them feel isolated and on the outside of main society

media broadcasting, publishing and the Internet

negative attitudes opinions or an outlook that is not optimistic but always looks on the dark or bad side of things

peers someone of your own age such as friends and classmates

pornography printed or visual material that shows or describes sexual activity

puberty the age or time when your body begins to develop and change into an adult body. The age for puberty to start is 8–14 years.

prejudice an unfair or unjust opinion which is not based on knowledge or experience

self-harming self-injury, deliberately hurting yourself

self-loathing hating yourself; feeling great dislike or disgust for yourself

sexual orientation the type of person someone is sexually attracted to, such as men, women or both

stereotype to fit someone into a specific group of people because of their looks, behaviour etc., which is not based on actual knowledge of the individual

surrogacy an agreement when a woman (called a surrogate mother) becomes pregnant and gives birth to a baby to give it to someone who cannot have children

testicles (also called testes or gonads) two round organs behind the penis that make sperm in men

tolerant showing willingness to accept opinions, beliefs or behaviour that are different from your own even when you may not agree with or approve of them

transgender a person whose personal identity and gender does not match the one given to them at birth

Further information

Note to parents and teachers: every effort has been made by the Publishers to ensure that these websites are suitable for children, that they are of the highest educational value, and that they contain no inappropriate or offensive material. However, because of the nature of the Internet, it is impossible to guarantee that the contents of these sites will not be altered. We strongly advise that Internet access is supervised by a responsible adult.

WEBSITES AND HELPLINES

If you feel overwhelmed by any of the issues you've read about or need advice, check out a website or helpline and talk to someone who will understand.

www.intercomtrust.org.uk
Online resources, community support and a confidential helpline for people of all ages in south-west England: 0800 612 3010

www.lgbtyouth.org.uk/young-people
Advice, information and online support based in Scotland. Call: 0131 555 3940
Text: 07786 202 370

www.itgetsbetter.org
A project to bring the LGBTQ community together locally and around the world and give them support.

www.themix.org.uk
A site for young people to get advice on a range of issues including emotions, sex and learning difficulties. Discussion boards, chat line.

www.childline.org.uk
Find out about issues that are troubling you, meet others, message or call the 24-hour helpline for advice or someone who'll just listen.
Helpline: 0800 1111.

www.supportline.org.uk
A charity giving emotional support to children and young people.

For readers in Australia and New Zealand

www.healthdirect.gov.au/partners/kids-helpline
A helpline for young people giving advice, counselling and support.

https://kidshelpline.com.au
Online and phone help for a wide range of issues.

www.kidsline.org.nz
Helpline run by young volunteers to help kids and teens deal with troubling issues and problems.

BOOKS AND OTHER STUFF

Two useful free pdf downloads from www.stonewall.org.uk:
Coming Out! answers some of the questions young people have about coming out, and questions about being lesbian, gay or bisexual. The guide offers advice, guidance and suggestions for further support.

Staying Safe Online is a guide for young people that looks at the risks you can face when using the Internet and social media.

Age of consent
The age of consent in the UK and parts of Australia is 16 for boys and girls, whatever their sexual orientation (in South Australia and Tasmania it is 17 years). In the UK it is illegal for anyone to have sex with a young person under the age of 16, or 18 (this varies in Australia) if the other person is an adult who has a position of care and trust, such as a social worker or teacher.

Index

adolescence 6, 7, 10
age of consent 23, 31
asexual 4
attraction 4, 7, 22

bullying 16, 17, 28

community 4, 16, 20, 27
consent 23, 31
culture 14

discrimination 16

family 14, 17, 18, 20, 21, 23, 24, 28
feelings 7, 10, 11, 14, 15, 16, 18, 20, 26, 27

gender 9

heterosexual 4, 12, 23
homophobia 16–17, 24

infatuation 10

media 4
moods 7

online safety 4, 7, 9, 31

pornography 22, 28
prejudice 12, 16, 24
puberty 6, 7

questioning 9

rainbow flag 12
relationships 4
religion 20–21, 28

same-sex crush 10-11
same-sex families 24–25, 28
sex 7, 22–23
sexual identity 4
sexual orientation 7, 10, 11, 22, 23, 26
stereotypes 12, 28

transgender 9

values 4

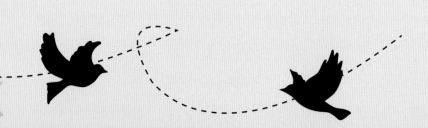

Fear of Failure

What is a fear of failure? • No one is born with a fear of failure • Making mistakes • Do you have a fear of failure? • High expectations • School stress • Friends for ever? • Self-esteem and failure • Make failure a success • Be inspired • What is *your* success? • Overcoming your fear

Cultural Issues

What is culture? • Culture and religion • Culture and law • A changing society • Stereotyping • Old v new • Clashes at home • Your rights matter • I am what I wear • Prejudice and discrimination • Dealing with prejudice • Respect!

Family Differences

A family today • Fighting families • Divorce • Single parent family • Trust and abuse • Manage your anger • Problems with siblings • Child carers • Living on the breadline • My life! • Family breakdown • Foster and adoption • Illness and death

Self-esteem and Confidence

What is self-esteem? • Body image • A healthy body image • You are unique • Being shy • What is self-confidence? • Pressure! • Being assertive • Learning difficulties • Bullied or bully?

Understanding Sexuality

Time for change • What is sexuality? • Being lesbian, gay or bisexual • Where do I fit in? • Setting the record straight • Coming out • Homophobia – it's not right • Dealing with bad feelings • Being accepted • Proud to be me!

Understanding Transgender

What is gender? • What is transgender? • Transgender is not LGB • Being me • Family support • Transitioning at school • Bullying and discrimination • Puberty – help! • Transitioning – the journey • Dan's story

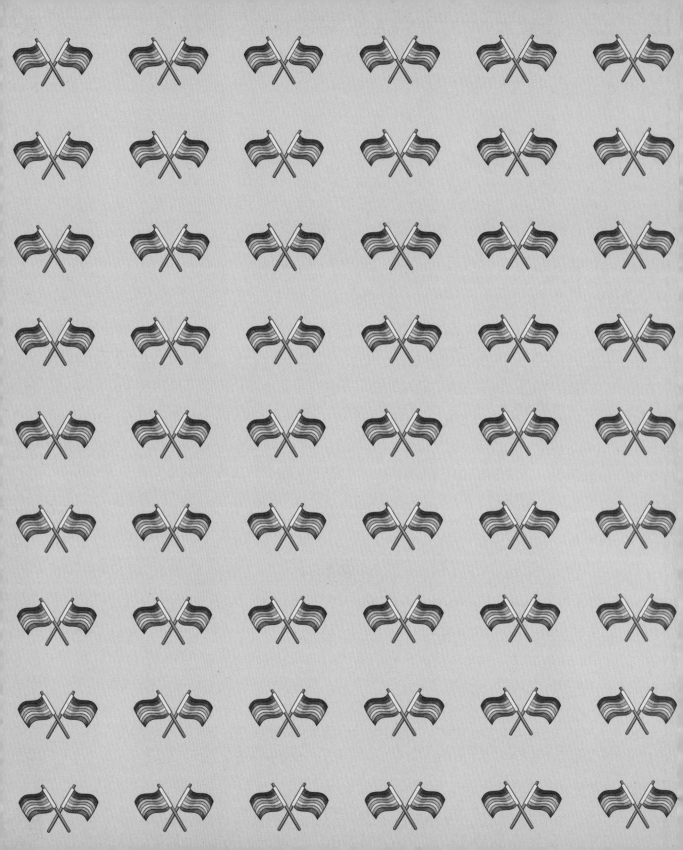